Accidental Inventions

Contents

Written by Jan Burchett and Sara Vogler

Illustrated by Katelyn McKenna

Collins

I'm Tamia and I'm a time-travelling reporter. Let's travel back in time to meet some people who've invented amazing things – by accident!

1 Accidental engineering inventions

Velcro

First, I'm investigating Velcro. Velcro is those two bits of fabric that hold

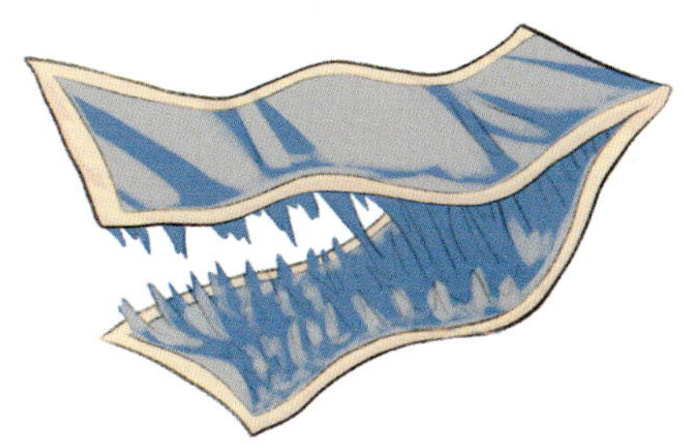

things together instead of buttons or zips. One side is rough and scratchy and the other is soft and fuzzy.

We all use it. You might even have Velcro on your shoes. It makes a great ripping noise when you pull it apart. But don't try this during a lesson!

Burdock seeds

Why are they sticking?
Who cares!

I'll look at this under my microscope.
What about me?

The seeds have little hooked spines!
And most of them are stuck to me!

This could be a new way of fastening things together.
How embarrassing!

After I'd got the seeds out of Milka's coat, I worked on my idea. Goodbye buttons and zips, I thought. There's a better way of fastening things – two strips of fabric, one with tiny hooks and the other with tiny loops. When they're put together, they'll stick fast. It took me ages to find a fabric strong enough to work. But by 1955, my new fastener was ready!

Velcro soon appeared all over the world ... and beyond! It is even used in space to keep things from floating about.

Here's a challenge. What could you invent with burdock seeds? Something to hang your socks on? A new game?

The word Velcro is made up from two French words: "velour" (velvet) and "crochet" (hook). Can you see how the word is made?

Fast fact – The Slinky

The Slinky was invented accidentally too.
In 1943, Richard James, an engineer, was working with some metal springs. He dropped one and was amazed to see it flipping across the floor. That is how the Slinky was born!

2 Accidental food inventions

Crisps

He says they're too thick.
I'll slice them as thin as paper.
Too mushy!
I'll fry them more.

Not enough salt.
I'll show him!
He says they're wonderful.

I called them Saratoga Chips and everyone loved them.
Who are you trying to kid, George? I invented Saratoga Chips.

Delicious!
Lovely and crispy.

You did not invent them!
I did too!
Yesterday you said you accidentally dropped a potato peeling into the fat and it crisped them up.
I did not!
You did too!

Brothers and sisters, eh! Will we ever know the real story? Of course, George Crum wasn't the first to fry potatoes in thin slices, but he was the one who made them popular. Or his sister did – who knows?

In 1817, William Kitchiner wrote a recipe for 'potatoes fried in slices or shavings'. Imagine going into a shop and asking for a packet of 'potatoes fried in slices or shavings'!

A challenge for you: think up a new crisp flavour. (No smelly feet or rotten sprouts!)

Do you know how ice lollies were invented? In about 1908, a boy called Frank Epperson made himself a drink using powdered lemonade, soda and water. He stirred it with a stick but then forgot it and left it outside on a very cold night. In the morning, the drink had frozen around the stick. He'd invented the ice lolly!

3 Accidental toy inventions

Play-Doh

Everyone loves Play-Doh. It's lovely and squidgy and smells nice. What's not to like?

We're rushing back to America again, this time to 20th century Cincinnati. We're meeting the inventors of Play-Doh, Noah McVicker and his nephew, Joseph.

Tell us about Play-Doh, Mr McVicker.

In the 1930s, I invented a putty to rub **soot** off wallpaper.

Why would people put soot on their wallpaper?

They didn't. Many people had coal fires in their houses. The smoke from burning coal makes soot and that's what made the walls dirty. So, people used my putty as a cleaner. But by 1950, lots of houses stopped using coal, and wallpaper could be wiped clean with water. No one needed my putty anymore.

What happened next?

My sister-in-law, Kay Zufall, is a teacher. She took some to her school.

I've got a new kind of clay for you to play with.

They really like it.

1956

We can sell our putty as play putty for kids!

16

It's dough that children play with. Let's call it Play-Doh.

1957
Let's make it in different colours.
Let's advertise it on TV.

Suddenly we were a worldwide success!

It's said that over 3 billion pots of Play-Doh have been sold. That's enough to reach the moon and back three times if they were stacked up!

What would you make with Play-Doh? What's the best thing you've ever made with Play-Doh?

Fast fact – The Super Soaker

In 1982, Lonnie Johnson, an engineer, was trying to invent a heat pump that ran on water. When a big jet of water shot out of it, he found he had invented a water blaster for children instead! He called it the Super Soaker.

4 Accidental medical inventions

Penicillin

Alexander should be back by now.
This is interesting.

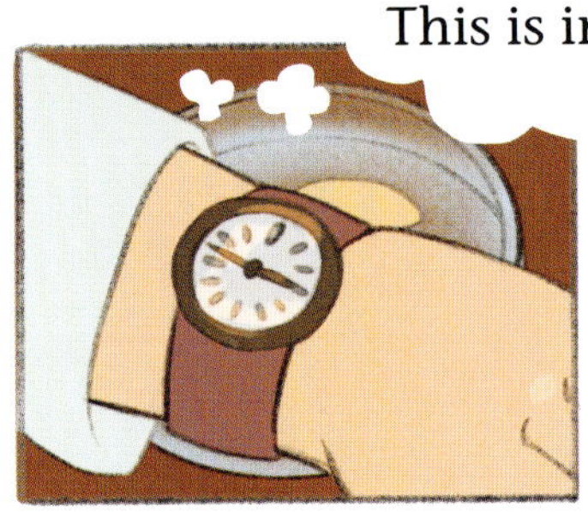

Welcome back! Look what I've found.

Whoops! I should have tidied away that dish of **bacteria** before my holiday.
But wait! There's mould growing.
That's strange!

Did you know?

Some ancient civilisations used to put mouldy bread on wounds to heal them. (Don't try this at home!)

I didn't give up and in 1943, with the help of scientists Howard Florey and Ernst Chain, I found a way to make big quantities of penicillin.

That was during the Second World War, wasn't it?

Yes, it came just in time for the men and women who were injured fighting.

Nobel Prize
for Medicine

It's thought that 500 million lives have been saved by penicillin. That's not bad coming from a dish of mould!

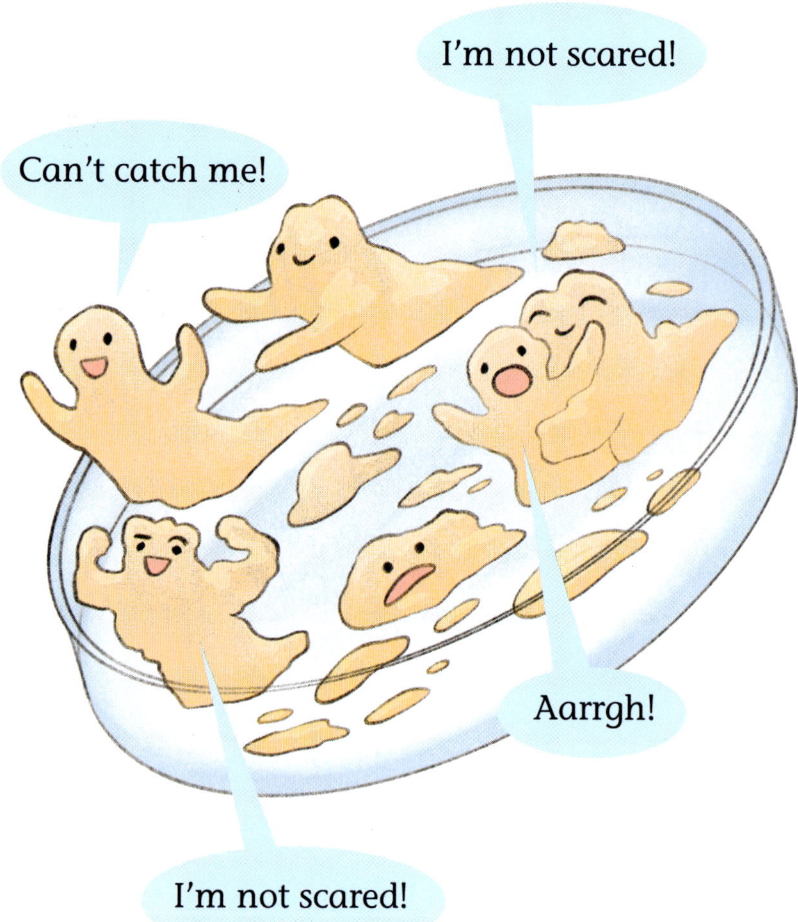

Here's a question for you: Which of these seven inventions do you think is the most exciting and why?

Glossary

antibiotics	medicine that kills bacteria
bacteria	tiny organisms that are everywhere around us – some are good but some can make us unwell
engineer	someone who works out the best way to create new things like engines, machines, buildings and bridges
laboratory	a place where scientists do experiments
microscope	a tool that magnifies tiny objects
Nobel Prize	an award given to people who have done something important in the world
scientist	a person who discovers new things and researches how things work
soot	a black powdery substance that is produced when coal or wood is burned

Index

Timeline

Talk about each invention.

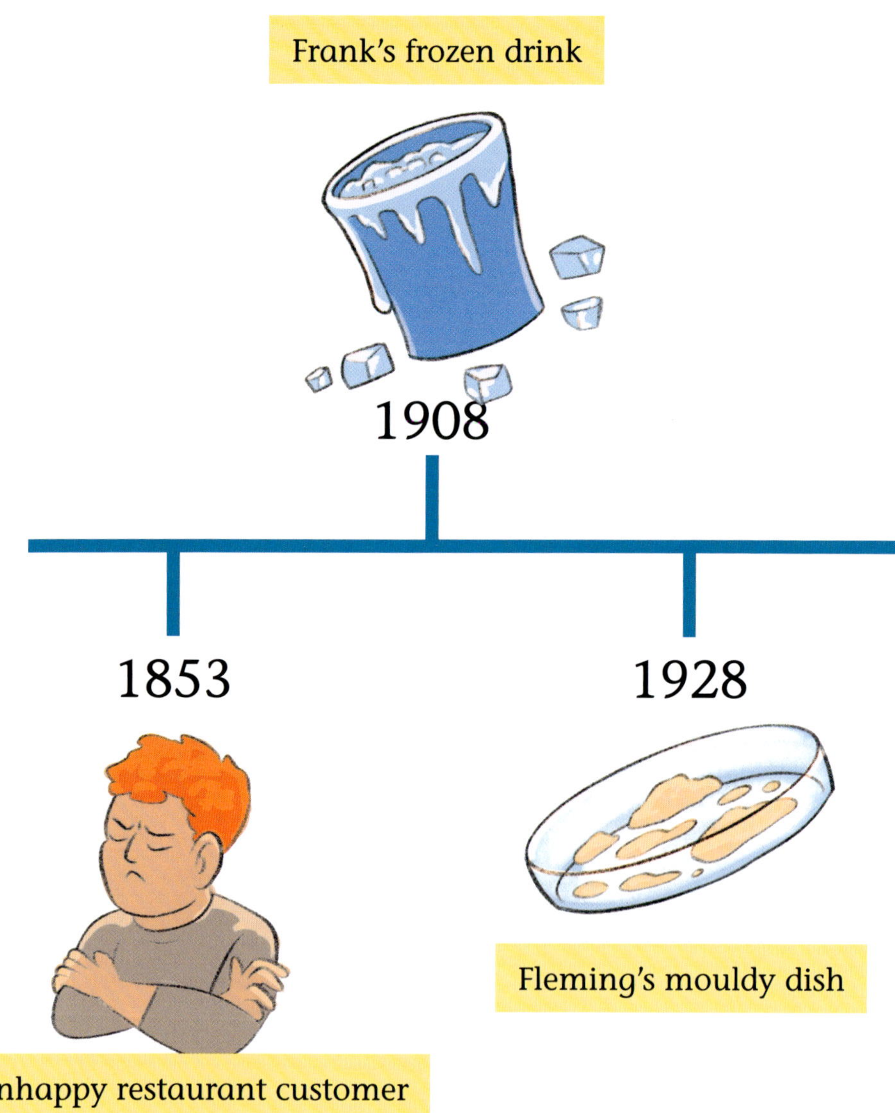

1941

1956

1943

1982

Ideas for reading

Written by Gill Matthews
Primary Literacy Consultant

Reading objectives:
- be introduced to non-fiction books that are structured in different ways
- draw on what they already know or on background information and vocabulary provided by the teacher
- check that the text makes sense to them as they read and correct inaccurate reading

Spoken language objectives:
- articulate and justify answers, arguments and opinions
- use spoken language to develop understanding through speculating, hypothesising, imagining and exploring ideas
- participate in discussions, presentations, performances, role play, improvisations and debates

Curriculum links: Science: Uses of everyday materials

Interest words: reporter, engineer, chef, teacher, doctor, scientist

Word count: 1453

Resources: ICT for research

Build a context for reading

- Ask children to look at the front cover of the book and to read the title.
- Explore their understanding of the title.
- Ask whether they can identify any of the objects shown on the cover and what they know about them.
- Read the back cover blurb. Discuss how an invention could be discovered by accident.
- Ask if they have an idea of what the man in the picture might be about to invent.
- Point out that this is an information book.
- Ask what features are often found in non-fiction texts.
- Challenge them to find the contents page. Discuss the purpose and organisation of a contents.